Forgive
The Glorious Face of Love

FORGIVENESS

THE GLORIOUS FACE
OF LOVE

by
**FRANCES
HOGAN**

Collins
FLAME

William Collins Sons & Co. Ltd

London • Glasgow • Sydney • Auckland

Toronto • Johannesburg

First published in Great Britain in 1990 by Flame

Flame is an imprint of
Collins Religious Division,
part of the Collins Publishing Group
8 Grafton Street, London W1X 3LA

Copyright © 1990 by Frances Hogan

Printed and bound in Great Britain by
Courier International Ltd, Tiptree, Essex

CONDITIONS OF SALE

Forgiveness: The Glorious Face Of Love

TO LOVE IS TO FORGIVE/
TO FORGIVE IS TO LOVE

When we witness a public example of forgiveness in the face of an evil deed we are deeply touched by such nobility of heart. Such was the case when a brave father went public in his forgiveness of those who killed his daughter at Enniskillen. So, too, when the Pope visited his would-be murderer in prison to extend to him his personal forgiveness. These acts show us *why* God asks us to forgive, for even the onlookers are ennobled by the deed, to say nothing of the participators, for how can we scream for revenge when the injured party lovingly forgives? Doesn't the sight somehow show us what it is to be truly human, and a child of God? Forgiveness is a case of overcoming evil with good, a demonstration that where sin abounds grace abounds even more (Rom. 5.21). Observing such acts of heroism liberates us from the sickening feeling that the world is run by evildoers, and that we are helpless in the face of such malice.

Forgiveness is the divine institution for dealing with injustice. It breaks the cycle of evil, of tit-for-tat revenge which serves only to increase the problem. It not only breaks the cycle of evil but also the power of evil, neutralizing its effects. It is the equivalent of taking the sword out of the enemies' hands and breaking it leaving them defenceless. Forgiveness is the liberating defence of the child of God. It is also one of the keys of the kingdom of Heaven, and those who use it know the joy of God's presence in their lives, and also of God's protection against all enemies both material and spiritual, for time and eternity.

When we buy a machine we normally get a manufacturer's handbook with it. This book carries instructions on the understanding and correct use of the machine. It also instructs the user on the procedure in case of breakdown or malfunction. And in the event of all else failing it provides the name, address and telephone number of the manufacturers. Our good God has provided us with a "manufacturer's handbook" in the sacred scriptures, in which the Creator and Redeemer of the human race tells His creatures how to behave so that they can live at the highest level of their being. It carries instructions on what to do when things go wrong and how to contact Him in prayer. In this booklet we want to address the subject of what to do when things go wrong, and in subsequent ones we will deal with prayer.

With regard to forgiveness Jesus said: "Be compassionate as your Father is compassionate. Do not judge, and you will not be judged yourselves; do not condemn, and you will not be condemned yourselves; grant pardon, and you will be pardoned. Give, and there will be gifts for you: a full measure, pressed down, shaken together, and running over, will be poured into your lap; because the amount you measure out is the amount you will be given back." Here the principles of successful living are spelled out. The Lord tells us that if we are compassionate we will never injure our neighbour, for compassion means that we look into the other person's eyes and both perceive and feel their pain. This enables us to be merciful.

As well as feeling the other's pain the Lord wants us to refrain from judging or condemning them, which means that we refuse to join the cycle of evil, and we also refuse – out of love – to increase their pain. We leave all justice and judgment to God ultimately, for He judges with fairness and full knowledge of all circumstances. Stepping outside of the cycle of evil altogether, we then pardon the guilty one so that the burden of their sin is not increased by the weight of our condemnation, which might make it impossible for them to recover or return to God. Jesus summarizes all this by saying, "Be a giver" to others, for then you will experience God's unlimited generosity to you in every sphere of life. Those who give pardon receive pardon easily: those who give understanding will be understood in time of need: those who refuse to condemn will not be condemned themselves. In other words you reap what you sow (Gal. 6.7–9, 5.13–24). To enter into judgment and condemnation, or worse still, revenge, is a case of sowing the wind to reap the whirlwind (Hos. 8.7).

EXAMPLES OF FORGIVENESS

There is nothing more wonderful than to be forgiven after doing wrong. It affects us deeply when someone tells us that we have been let off the hook, that there will be no more about it, and that they continue their friendship as if nothing had happened. One instinctively knows that one is loved, and moreover that that love is unmerited. We have experienced *mercy*, a truly divine gift. Let us look at some examples of it and then go on to explore this wonderful gift that God asks us to give to others who have offended us.

First, let us look at King David who lived one thousand years before Christ, and who, therefore, did not have the graces and opportunities granted to us who live in the era of divine mercy. David lived under the covenant of Moses which was much more severe than the law of Christ which is all about love, both human and divine. Under the old covenant one was expected to do away with one's enemies, not to have mercy and forgive them, which is such a characteristic of Christ (Matt. 5.44). The old law followed the *Lex Talionis* "An eye for an eye and a tooth for a tooth" (Ex. 21.24).

Our stories are in I Samuel 24 and 26 where David is on the run from King Saul, not because of any fault on his part, but because of Saul's insane jealousy of David's giftedness generally and also because of his success in war (I Sam. 18.6–10). Saul was determined to kill David by his own hand, so he pursued him relentlessly throughout Israel for years. As king he could so easily have paid a hit man to do the job, but he preferred to do it himself instead of getting on with ruling his country. This frenzy to kill David consumed him and drove him to search the country continuously for David, who was, by then, denied all human rights. Things got so bad that it was dangerous to try to help David for your life would be forfeit, as happened to the priests of Nob (I Sam. 21.1–9, 22.6–23). The situation became too dangerous even for his family, who had to be left with the King of Moab (I Sam. 22.1–4).

In this context, and considering that we are dealing with 1,000 years before Christ, we could expect that David would desire only revenge on his enemy. But it was not so. Saul, returning from engaging the Philistines in battle, went with a force of 3,000 men to find poor David who was hiding in the recesses of a cave at Engedi, near the Dead Sea. It so happened that Saul went unaccompanied into the same cave to ease himself, thus unwittingly putting himself in David's power. David's men urged him to take revenge, for such a golden opportunity might not come again, yet he refused. Instead, he sneaked up behind the king and cut off a small piece of the king's cloak as evidence of his mercy. When Saul left the cave David followed him, called, and showed the piece of cloth publicly before the assembled army as proof of his forbearance and forgiveness.

Saul was deeply touched. He wept aloud saying: "You are a more upright man than I, for you have repaid me good while I repaid you evil. Today you have crowned your goodness towards me since the Lord had put me in your power yet you did not kill me. When a man comes on his enemy, does he let him go unmolested? May the Lord reward you for the goodness you have shown me today." Whereupon Saul begged David to swear that he would never cut off Saul's descendants when he came to the throne. David took the oath and kept it (see 2 Sam. 9.1–13).

I Samuel 26 gives yet another example of David trying to touch the heart of his enemy with forgiveness and mercy, for Saul had learned nothing, and had not allowed David to return home after the last incident. He was still an outlaw. Saul was again searching for David to kill him, but David outwitted him. He entered the king's tent during the night as the army camped out in the open. He quietly stole Saul's sword from beside his head as he slept in his tent surrounded by his sleeping bodyguards! Then going out again David aroused the army from sleep by calling the king. He showed the evidence of his mercy and forbearance yet again, for the sword revealed that David had been inside the king's tent and had still left him unmolested.

This time the forgiveness brought a confession of sin

from Saul, but unfortunately for himself and everyone associated with him, it did not bring about a change of heart. Saul replied: "I have sinned. Come back, my son David; I will never harm you again since you have shown such respect for my life today. Yes, my course has been folly and my error grave." And David was blessed by his mortal enemy, for human beings are deeply moved by the nobility of forgiveness, even when they are as sick in mind and spirit as Saul was at that time.

THE FORGIVENESS OF JOSEPH

The Book of Genesis also furnishes a moving tale of forgiveness in the story of the patriarch Joseph, who suffered untold injustice from his own family, being sold into slavery just because his brothers were jealous of his giftedness (Gen. 37). To add insult to injury, when he was doing well at his job as the slave steward of Potiphar in Egypt, he found himself thrown into prison because of unjust accusations on the part of Potiphar's lustful wife.

It seemed he would spend the rest of his life in jail for he had no one to take his part or plead his cause. He was one of the poor who only have God to turn to, and if God is not just and kind they have no hope. Joseph never heard Psalm 34, which was written centuries later, yet he experienced what that psalmist wrote: "A cry goes up from the poor man, and the Lord hears, and helps him in all his troubles" (v. 6). "The Lord is near to the broken hearted, He helps those whose spirit is crushed" (v. 18). "Hardships in plenty beset the virtuous man, but the Lord rescues him from them all" (v. 19). If Joseph could not master the lesson of

forgiveness he was not only doomed to rot in prison, but he would have the added misery of bitterness, hatred, and a desire for revenge that would do nothing but destroy his own spirit.

Yet that did not happen, for we are continuously told throughout the tale that "the Lord was with Joseph" (Gen. 39.2, 5, 21). It seemed that he was doomed to a terrible fate; that life had served him a poor hand, but it was not so. This was the schooling that made Joseph the man of God that he became, and it turned him into the first saviour of Israel. God raised him high, second only to Pharaoh, and gave this wonderful servant, who learned to forgive and trust God in all circumstances, the great task of saving the starving poor of the world in his own day, and he was the only man with the wisdom of God to handle the situation (Gen. 40, 41 esp. vv. 38–39). Joseph learned the wisdom of forgiveness, and through prayer he got the strength from God to endure, and triumph over all adverse circumstances.

It was the famine that drove Joseph's brothers to Egypt in search of food. They who had shown no mercy to their young brother now beg him for food for their whole tribe (Gen. 42.21). Joseph recognized them, but they did not recognize him since they were convinced that he was dead. Under these circumstances Joseph had an ideal opportunity for revenge. It would have been so easy to get even. Would Joseph repay evil with evil? How great must have been the temptation since they were at his mercy! But no. He was a man of God. He merely worked on them to get his brother Benjamin to come to Egypt so that he could slowly become acquainted with his family again. His forgiveness of his brothers was truly heroic. He acknowledged that God had transformed his misery into glory: "Do not grieve, do not reproach yourselves for having sold me here, since God sent me here before you to preserve your lives . . . so it was not you who sent me here, but God . . . and he kissed all his brothers weeping over them" (Gen. 45.1–15).

Joseph repaid his brothers good instead of evil, and he it was who brought Israel to Egypt as the guests of the great potentate Pharaoh who would do anything for his great servant Joseph (Gen. 46, 47). As long as the pharaohs remembered Joseph all was well for the tribes of Israel in Egypt. Joseph's forgiveness was the key to opening Egypt to Israel. Forgiveness on the part of his descendants might have changed their subsequent history, for forgiveness is the key to opening all doors on Planet Earth. It is also one of the keys to the kingdom of heaven, for it opens the door to salvation, as we shall see.

NEW TESTAMENT EXAMPLES OF FORGIVENESS

One of the most touching examples of forgiveness in the New Testament is that of the first martyr Stephen in Acts 7. Stephen is described as an ideal disciple of Jesus in Acts 6.5–7.15; He was a man full of faith and full of the Holy Spirit; also filled with grace and power, working miracles and great signs among the people. He was also a dynamic preacher, full of wisdom because he allowed the Lord to govern all that he said and did. It is not difficult to see that envy and jealousy would get to work on such a person, especially from those in ministry who were failing God in all the ways that Stephen served Him.

Stephen was arrested secretly and taken for trial

before the same Sanhedrin that had tried his Master without pity or justice, so the disciple would know that he could expect the same treatment that his Master received. In fact Stephen's trial was an exact replica of Jesus' one, for the Sanhedrin procured false witnesses to testify against him by twisting his teaching in such a way that it could be construed that he had blasphemed against the Temple. It was one thing for Jesus to triumph personally over such injustice, but could a weak creature like ourselves do the same?

The answer is a resounding yes! Jesus had promised that when he had triumphed over sin, death and Hell for us that His disciples would be able to do the same works as He did Himself because he would be at the Father's side making intercession for us (John 14.12). Stephen was standing before this unjust human court, but he raised the eyes of his soul to the Supreme Court of Heaven and beheld Jesus in vision at the right hand of the Father and knew that all that had been promised would be fulfilled. Thus he could endure this disastrous trial and the summary execution that followed it. Before he died Stephen imitated his Master for the last time on earth by dying with the same words of Jesus on his lips: "'Lord Jesus receive my spirit.' Then he knelt down and said aloud, "'Lord do not hold this sin against them', and with these words he fell asleep in death."

The text tells us that Saul (later Paul) entirely approved of the killing (Acts 8.1). But that was not the end of the matter, for this glorious death haunted Saul, preparing his soul for the dramatic conversion he had later when he became the great missionary of the Master for whom Stephen had given his life. There is no doubt that the martyr's blood pleaded for the salvation of the persecutor's soul, thus cancelling out the evil and creating an even greater good, for Saul would himself become the untiring preacher of Jesus, and leave behind the testimony of a great harvest won for the Lord, many writings of unsurpassed wisdom, and the final witness of a life laid down for the Master. He, too, became a martyr for Jesus. Stephen had not died in vain, for Paul was part of Stephen's harvest for God. This is yet another example of the fact that God works very differently from us, and that it is so hard for us to even fathom His ways (Isa. 55.6–9; Rom. 11.33–36). It also demonstrates the miracle-working power of forgiveness.

There are other examples of forgiveness too, in the missionary work of the apostles, who, instead of being thanked for the work they did for people, were persecuted everywhere they went, yet they never held a grudge against anyone for the dreadful treatment meted out to them. The Sanhedrin in Jerusalem persecuted them as long as they remained there (Acts 4 & 5), yet they merely grew stronger as a result of the persecution. Not only would they not waste their precious life-energy on the negativity of bitterness or resentment, but they were happy to suffer for the name of Jesus, and they prayed that God would give them more boldness in preaching and teaching, and multiply the signs that proved that Jesus was risen and gloriously present, though unseen in their midst (Acts 4.23–31).

Their reaction to hurt was so triumphant that it paralysed their enemies, the best of whom had to admit that in persecuting these disciples they could be fighting against God Himself (Acts 5.39). The Christian missionaries have continued their triumphant march through history and no enemy has succeeded in wiping them out, for the enemy does not understand that forgiveness is an unassailable fortress defended by God Himself.

THE PROBLEM OF UNFORGIVENESS

The problem of unforgiveness is all too common, and it has many guises. Some people turn-in on themselves nursing a grudge or resentment for years on end, turning the matter over and over in their minds until it reaches huge proportions. Yet they may never say anything to the party concerned, so that the problem remains unsolved. In the meantime the offender may have forgotten the incident, and consequently cannot understand why the other person is so resentful and bitter, and so impossible to live with, maybe for a whole lifetime.

This is utterly tragic, and a waste of a human life, for we cannot be positive and creative about life while nursing such negative thoughts in our hearts. Negativity cancels out creativity, and so the one who nurses resentment harms themselves *more* than the offender did in the first place. Many people are their own worst enemy, for they hold themselves bound by past events that they never let go of, and thus they spoil the possibility of enjoying present relationships, and the joy of even *handling* life properly.

Life must be very confined and confining if every time we are hurt we store that hurt away and cut the offender off our list of relationships. We would eventually end up a prisoner in our own home, or worse still, in our own mind, or go mad altogether. This can be the beginning of a deep depression or mental breakdown, both of which are often associated with unforgiven hurts. There is no point in going to a psychiatric hospital for a "magic cure" when confession and forgiveness can bring about healing of hurts with no financial cost. The healing of memories through prayer is so effective in this matter, and can bring not only total relief, but wipe out even the memory altogether, leaving one completely free.

Forgiveness is one of the keys to handling life successfully, whereas unforgiveness is a case of putting the noose around one's own neck to choke off all possibility of experiencing *real* love. Forgiveness is an expression of love that makes it possible to continue a relationship after a problem has arisen, or an offence has been given. If that forgiveness is withheld then the offender is held bound and the relationship is thereby blocked. The ball is in the court of the offended one, who can block real living from now on just by refusing this wonderful sign of love to one they *say* that they love. There is *no love* if forgiveness is lacking, because it means that the so-called love is conditional on certain behaviour. We must look at our responsibility here, for Jesus said: "If you forgive men's sins, they are forgiven them; if you hold them bound, they are held bound" (John 20–23).

We must now look at the effect of this refusal to forgive. Jesus said that if we here on earth hold a person bound in their sin they are held bound in Heaven. In other words we hold them for judgment. What a frightful thing! We would not like anyone to do that to us! Don't we all hope that the things we have done to others will be forgotten? Don't we feel hurt when someone lets us know that they *remember* our faults? Isn't there a sense of bitterness when we realize that someone refuses to forgive us? Does it make us friendly towards them, or negative? Does it enhance or block relationship? If we know the pain of being

unforgiven surely we will understand Jesus' command to forgive! Unforgiveness blocks life, blocks relationships, and, as we shall see later, it effectively blocks prayer and the possibility of healing from the Lord. It can be called "spiritual cholesterol" which blocks up the channels of life and causes spiritual heart attacks and the possibility of spiritual death. And it is all so unnecessary, when God gives us the grace to forgive. What we cannot do of ourselves He makes possible.

Forgiveness must be given not only by individuals, but also by groups who find themselves in opposition, like the apartheid problem everywhere. So also must the various groups who call themselves Christians, but who oppose and condemn each other on doctrinal grounds. Forgiveness and reconciliation would bring about the miracle of the healing of the Body Of Christ in the world, a fact that would occasion great renewal and restoration to the Church. Nations, too, must forgive if we are not to continue destroying ourselves in world wars. Forgiveness would bring about international cooperation on all levels instead of the factions on national and international level that destroy trade as well as good relations. You will say that this is too idealistic. Listen to the lament of Psalm 2, which is fulfilled when revenge and selfishness rule the world:

Why this uproar among the nations?
Why this impotent muttering of pagans –
kings on earth rising in revolt,
princes plotting against the Lord and his Anointed,
"Now let us break their fetters!
Now let us throw off their yoke!"

The rest of the psalm shows that warring and rebellious nations force the hand of God to come in judgment to restore order and the law of God, which alone brings peace. Thus we have in our own hands the power to have a world at peace or at war. It is exactly what Moses said to the Israelites in the desert: "Today I set before you life and prosperity, or death and disaster . . . choose life then!" (Deut. 30.15–20)

THE CURSE OF REVENGE

While some people nurse resentment against offenders and remain negative, but outwardly inactive, others resort to revenge. They are determined to get even, so they become judge, jury and law officers, deciding to deal with the offender according to their own rules. This spells disaster, for there will be no justice, and most certainly no mercy, for the revenge taken is very often out of all proportion to the offence. Retaliation or revenge is forbidden by the Lord. Leviticus 19.18: "Do not seek revenge or bear a grudge against one of your people, but love your neighbour as yourself. I am the Lord". Proverbs 20:22: "Do not say, 'I'll pay you back for this wrong!' Wait for the Lord and he will deliver you." Romans 12:17: "Do not repay anyone evil for evil. Be careful to do what is right in the eyes of everybody". I Peter 3:9: "Do not repay evil with evil, or insult with insult, but with blessing, because to this you were called so that you may inherit a blessing".

The scriptures provide us with examples of revenge because all scripture is given to us for our learning, and we must learn what not to do from looking at these examples given (2 Tim. 3.15–17). We have the case of the infamous Jezebel in I Kings 19 who decided to kill the prophet Elijah because, on Mount Carmel, he had dealt with the false prophets who brought apostasy and immorality to the nation. She swore an oath that in 24 hours Elijah himself would be killed by her agency. But he did not die for the Lord protected him.

The infamous Herodias in the Gospel took violent revenge on John the Baptist by beheading him at a birthday party! And this because the Lord's servant asked for her repentance in order to bring her salvation (Matt. 14.3–12). The Nazarenes took revenge on Jesus by trying to kill Him because He claimed to be the Messiah, but yet could do no miracles among them because of their unbelief (Luke 4.29). Later the Jews of the Dispersion took an oath to kill Paul because they said that his missionary work was harming them (Acts 23.12).

Just as the examples of forgiveness above left us with a good feeling, and a sense of being ennobled, so these examples which have been related so briefly, leave us with a bad feeling. The odour of sanctity flows from the forgiveness group, and the stench of wickedness comes from these, thus revealing to us that forgiveness is a fruit of the Spirit and revenge has its source in Hell, and makes hell for others. There can be no justice where revenge reigns. One can only pity its victims, for no good can come of it, unless the victim can overcome the evil with their heroic forgiveness as in Stephen's case, cited above.

THE LOVING MERCY OF JESUS

Examples of Jesus' forgiveness and mercy abound in the gospel. The passages relating these events are often our favourite readings because they reveal the heart of God so wonderfully to us, and make us feel confident in His presence and more able to come to Him with our own troubles. Let us take the example of the woman taken in adultery in John 8.1–11. This is a wonderful story which has an Old Testament counterpart in the story of the innocent Susanna in Daniel 13. Susanna's case was that of an innocent victim being brought to execution because of the revenge of two frustrated rapists. Because of her innocence she could call on God's justice to come to her aid. The Lord heard her cry and stirred up the spirit of prophecy in young Daniel, who exposed the truth. Thus the innocent woman was set free, and the punishment about to be given to her was, in fact, given to her two enemies. Susanna was vindicated.

Susanna's story leaves one delighted at the justice of God on the one hand, and with an uneasy feeling on the other, for how many of us could *afford* to pray for justice? Certainly a sinner could not! Justice is the last thing a sinner needs, since Psalm 49.7–9 says that "man could never redeem himself or pay his ransom to God: it costs so much to redeem his life, it is beyond him". So if we only had Susanna's story it would give little consolation to sinners.

This is precisely where the other story comes in, for in it we are dealing with a woman who committed the sin for which Susanna was accused. Did God find a way for the guilty to approach Him too? The answer is "Yes!" for He revealed to Moses at the beginning of the spiritual journey of the Chosen People that He was "The Lord, a God of tenderness and compassion, slow to anger, rich in kindness and faithfulness; for thousands he maintains his kindness, forgives faults, transgressions, sin; yet he lets nothing go unchecked . . . ." (Exodus 34:6–8).

The way to heaven for sinners is through the gate of God's infinite mercy, which is undeserved love. It is this undeserved love that is found in John 8 which is so beautiful to observe. A group of men took this woman

24

to Jesus saying that they had caught her in the very act of committing adultery, which of course means that they were hidden in her bedroom! They had set a trap for the poor woman who was now destined to be the victim of their unfounded zeal for the letter of the Law, for they wanted to stone her to death. They asked Jesus to pronounce judgment.

He was to be the New Daniel, and expose the truth. In this, of course, they were setting a trap for Jesus also, for Rome had removed the right to execute from the Sanhedrin. They already knew Jesus' mercy for sinners, and they wanted an excuse to hand him over to either the Sanhedrin if he spoke against the Law or to the Roman authorities if he initiated the execution. The poor woman is merely a pawn in this cruel game set up also to trap Jesus. The revenge of these men is horrible, for neither the woman's life nor that of Jesus is of any value to them. They don't care if both lives are forfeit.

The New Daniel went into action as the Finger of God writing to the dust of the earth (a symbol of man, whose name is "dust", Adamah) regarding its sinfulness. Thus, delicately, Jesus allowed the men to know that He considered *them* guilty, since they conspired to catch the woman, and they now conspire to kill her – and Jesus! Jesus insisted that if the Law of Moses were to be imposed, it would be imposed *properly* which meant that the judge had to be *without* sin! And Jesus had just exposed their sin, so if they wished to avoid His judgment they had to leave, which they did! He was so merciful to them. He did not condemn these men, but gave them an opportunity to repent, and in so doing he also saved their victim.

Jesus had been the only one present without sin, but instead of stoning the woman He forgave her. This does not mean that he condoned the sin, but that He gave her an opportunity to begin again living a new and decent life worthy of herself, and of her status as a child of God. "Jesus looked up and said, 'woman, where are they? Has no one condemned you?' 'No one, sir', she replied. 'Neither do I condemn you', said Jesus. 'Go away and don't sin any more' " (John 8.11). The delicacy of Jesus here is lovely. The woman has nothing to fear in His presence. Her person and her life are both safe, and eternal life is offered too. He asks her to live, and love, in a worthy way.

THE COMMAND TO FORGIVE

Not everyone is called upon to forgive heroically, but all are commanded to forgive. Jesus says in Matthew 6.14: "Yes if you forgive others their failings, your heavenly Father will forgive you yours; but if you do not forgive others, your Father will not forgive your failings either". And in Luke 17:4 He says: "If your brother does something wrong reprove him and, if he is sorry, forgive him. And if he wrongs you seven times a day and seven times comes back to you and says 'I am sorry', you must forgive him".

First of all Jesus presents us with a two-edged sword by trying God's forgiveness of us on to our forgiveness of others! Nasty isn't it? God knows His creatures very well, and He therefore knows how unjust we are, wanting forgiveness for ourselves but not so keen to pass this gift of life on to others, so He ties both of them together, and makes them conditional each on the other. Is there anything more that a sinner needs than God's forgiveness? Without it there is no salvation! We are doomed to Hell, which is the eternal loss of God's presence and love. This means the utter, complete frustration of our being, no matter what "material" form it takes!

Listen to a paraphrase of Psalm 130: "Lord I cry to you from the depths of my sinfulness and my unbelief; from the deep abyss of fallen human nature which craves for pleasure, money and power, the three great idolatries. Lord, you must hear me! Oh! listen compassionately to one who can name the problem but can do nothing to resolve it without your forgiveness. Lord I am horrified when I look at myself. I am horrible in my own eyes. What must I be like before your gaze which is so holy? Please do not look at my faults, oh Lord, otherwise I will not be able to withstand your Presence. Have mercy on me, since you *are* Mercy, and I believe on your Word. My soul, wounded and depressed, confides and relies in you, and in your promises. From dawn till dusk, that is from my youth till my old age I will hope in you."

Anyone who has faced their own need of God's forgiveness would find it an intolerable burden if God would not forgive us, for the weight of our guilt would enslave us for eternity. We would hate God if there was *nothing* that could make us right in His sight. It would draw the very worst traits from us, and we would become veritable satans, vindictive, and dedicated to evil. Moreover, we would accuse God of being *unjust* since He in fact, was the only One who could get us out of the fix we got ourselves into. It is absolutely essential for the continuance of the human race that God would be merciful and forgive. For if He would not forgive, how could we expect anyone else to do so? And life on earth without forgiveness would be a veritable hell, and definitely not worth living.

So it is imperative that God should forgive. Psalm

103 celebrates God's forgiving love, and compares it to the tenderness of a father who understands the foibles of his tiny ones.

Bless the Lord, my soul,
and remember all his kindnesses:
in forgiving all your offences,
in curing all your diseases,
in redeeming your life from the pit,
in crowning you with love and tenderness,
in filling your years with prosperity,
in renewing your youth like an eagle's.

The Lord is tender and compassionate,
slow to anger, most loving;
his indignation does not last forever,
his resentment exists a short time only;
he never treats us, never punishes us,
as our guilt and our sins deserve.

No less than the height of heaven over earth
is the greatness of his love for those who fear him;
he takes our sins further away
than the east is from the west.

As tenderly as a father treats his children,
so the Lord treats those who fear him;
he knows what we are made of,
he remembers we are dust . . .

Even when we have sinned greatly – as distinct from the ordinary everyday falls – we still expect God to understand and forgive. We still expect Him to forget!

An example of this was when King David sinned greatly although God had blessed him greatly in so many ways. As a result of his sexual greed he brought a woman down in adultery, and tried to cloak his sin by murdering her husband "legitimately" in war. Because of this David's nearest neighbours lost their reputation, their lives, their property – which would have reverted to the crown. They lost their right to their own lives, their privacy, and their own spouses, just because of one man's greed! When the sin was presented to David delicately cloaked in a parable, he said that the man who committed such foul deeds ought to die! It was the prophet Nathan's unpleasant task to inform him that *he* was that filthy, lousy sinner! What we can see quite clearly in someone else's case is much more difficult to see in our own (2 Samuel 11, 12).

Yet, as soon as David acknowledged his sin he *expected* God to understand and forgive him! His prayer is found in Psalm 51 where he asks God for tender mercy, something he was not prepared to give his neighbours! He pleaded weakness and original sin as mitigating factors and said that he was born a sinner, and therefore God should understand such weakness. Yet he showed no mercy or understanding to his wounded neighbours who were very weak before a great potentate like David. They had no court of appeal when the highest in the land was their enemy. Isn't it strange that we expect from God what we refuse to our neighbours? Is this just?

Nathan mediated God's forgiveness, His unmerited absolution and loving kindness to David in 2 Samuel 12.14. It was this unlimited, undeserved love of God that broke David, for he knew that any person coming before him under these circumstances would have been summarily executed without mercy. But God is different. He would rather a *living* repentant sinner to a dead unrepentant one, because such a one would have lost salvation, for "God wants everyone to be saved and to reach full knowledge of the truth" (I Tim. 2.5). It was this divine wisdom that made David go and repent properly, as is seen in Psalm 51. He then understood that he needed deep cleansing from God if he were not to repeat the crime.

True repentance in our own lives furnishes us with the wisdom required to truly forgive others. Let us listen to Paul in Colossians 3.13: "Bear with one another; forgive each other as soon as a quarrel begins. The Lord has forgiven you; now you must do the same." Paul was one of those sinners who had been forgiven much, so he taught the justice of passing on that forgiveness to others. He also provided the true motivation for forgiveness, especially for those occasions when we feel that it costs too much. We are to remember that God has forgiven us when we least deserved it.

To prevent a big crisis between people from brewing up to storm force, Paul advises in Ephesians 4.32: "Be friends with one another, and kind, forgiving each other as readily as God forgave you, in Christ." So Paul, like Jesus, expects us to keep our grace up to date! For if we deal with today's problems today, we will avoid that big bust-up that few are able to face. Having that big row very often produces more heat than light, and so the energy generated is of no use in building relationships. Instead it often produces accusations out of all proportion to reality, which only increases the level of hurt, and the difficulty of reaching a solution.

UNREASONABLE FORGIVENESS?

Once the subject of forgiveness is brought up we all produce situations where we claim that forgiving that person in those circumstances would only increase the problem, and so our forgiveness could in fact be feeding the problem instead of solving it. Let us address this aspect of forgiveness that seems to us unreasonable. Luke put it well when he said that if someone hurt you seven times a day and seven times came back and said "sorry" that we are to forgive them. Is there anyone who believes that this is reasonable behaviour? Is there anyone prepared to experiment with this principle? Don't we walk off saying that we can't be fanatics! . . . nor dopes! Surely Jesus does not demand that we allow people to walk all over us? and misuse us? Surely not!

The case that Luke is dealing with involves a person *really trying* to overcome something, but they keep failing . . . and they keep repenting! It is also a private matter involving only two people, so it is ordinary faults that are at stake. In that situation Luke says "Be like God", for that is the way God behaves towards all His creatures. Luke 6.36 fits in here: "Be merciful, as your heavenly Father is merciful". Luke says that we should do for this repentant sinner what parents do for children who keep making mistakes in learning, and the loving parents patiently correct them, help them, affirm and love them until they become independent and proficient at whatever is the problem. This poor sinner may be trying to overcome their bad temper, which seems to get worse instead of getting better. They may be trying to control their tongue and apologize each time they fail. Help them instead of criticizing them!

Even to laugh instead of taking the whole matter too seriously would release the tension in the situation, and may even cure the problem.

Ah! can I hear you say that this does not represent *all* cases? What about those who appear to be incorrigible, who need to be taught a lesson? Am I not just exposing myself to being used or abused by someone who has no intention of changing? What about the case when I run into a "brick wall"? Certain problems in the home do need to be addressed if young lives are not to be ruined, and afflicted spouses face an early grave from stress and sustained tension over long periods of time. Such is the case in families where addictive or compulsive behaviour is manifested. Such is the case of abnormal psychological behaviour that requires professional help, so that a family is not subjected to mental torture, or emotional manipulation in all its various guises.

Does forgiveness cover all this? Yes! Then does forgiveness mean that you don't face the real problem and deal with it? No! Forgiveness is not a case of running away from reality, but of facing reality with the help of divine grace, so that the best solution can be found for all parties concerned. Forgiveness makes it possible for that solution to be offered without negativity, or vindictiveness of any kind. In other words it is an important manifestation of love, real love, that prefers to suffer for the good of the other party. Loving another person in time of need often entails suffering to all parties concerned until the healing is found, and then true peace enters into the situation, which settles down.

What motivates us to act to find a solution to a problem is often the pain we feel regarding it, or the bad effects produced by the problem manifesting itself.

But forgiveness does not exist *in the feelings*, it exists in the *will* of the person graced by God. The feelings may be very hurt, the emotions may be very bruised, but the will agrees to cooperate with God's way of doing things, so that no personal vendetta is carried out. No revenge is taken, and no tit-for-tat hurts. To behave thus is to be part of the problem, and such behaviour can only worsen things, until life becomes hell for all concerned.

To forgive means *to choose* to hold that person *without judgment* in love and prayer, and to *assist them* in every way possible towards a solution. Sometimes this involves action; sometimes silence, depending on circumstances. Once the will, aided by grace, agrees to forgive, the person has stepped outside the arena of evil and can assist in the solution. On a psychological level this releases a burden of tension and guilt off the offender, giving them a clearer mind to face facts. It is hard to face anything under a cloud of accusations and suspicions.

The removal of judgment, accusation, suspicion, and revenge changes the atmosphere in the house significantly, and makes a way for the Lord to come in and act on your behalf as Saviour. It makes it easier for the offender to *hear* what has to be said, and frees them somewhat to respond. It also removes one of their excuses, which is *your behaviour* towards them! And so it isolates the problem more. It uncomplicates the issues to be handled; it begins the unravelling process. It also means that *your prayer* on behalf of that person can now be heard because unforgiveness blocks prayer completely, making it useless. God is love, and only prayer made in love makes an impression on love. Love is the environment for healing, and the prerequisite for miracles. Do you need a miracle in your situation? Then forgive, and face reality *in love*. Pray through love, and the Divine Love will hear you.

STRUGGLING TO FORGIVE

Life provides us with plenty of opportunities to become proficient in forgiveness. People often hurt us without even being aware of it. Others are so wrapped up in themselves that they do not notice their behaviour affects you deeply in a negative way. Yet again, there are those poor souls who are spiteful and mean, and relationships with them border on the impossible, and this without taking into account recognized abnormal patterns of behaviour.

Marriage can be destroyed when people think that their adult life should be governed by reactions they gave to parents in the distant past, so that present spouses become aware that they are not even persons, but mere representations of childhood problems. In this way a wife can be translated "mother", or a husband "father", or even "authority figure", and they are not allowed to be themselves at all. And of course it is not possible to verbalize the myriad permutations and combinations of all sorts of unsolved problems that complicate personal relationships and render marriage a most difficult challenge for anyone who wants to be their own person instead of being shoved into a pattern of behaviour alien to them. It is so very urgent for us to get our act together in this essential area of personal relationships, since our own happiness, and the welfare of our children, depend on it, let alone the survival of marriage itself.

Forgiveness is not magic, and it does not produce

magical effects. It is a costly way of handling life that brings about the ultimate good of each person involved in a situation. It can only be operated by someone who loves, and who is prepared to bear the cost of loving in a challenging situation. Therefore do not expect that one little act of forgiveness will transform your spouse or your misbehaving teenager! Some people can put up quite a resistance, becoming worse before they begin to change for the better. This is because forgiveness is part of spiritual warfare and the great enemy of souls, Satan, does not *want* this situation resolved, because his business is to *create hell* both now, during our lifetime, and also hereafter. So many families who do not believe in a hell hereafter are experiencing it now. What a deception! What a disaster!

Both heaven and hell can be, and are experienced now, everywhere in society. The signs of heaven are love, joy and peace, affirmation, cooperation, trust and self-sacrificing service. Whereas the signs of hell are the absence of love, the presence of strife, condemnation, judgement, revenge, suspicion, the absence of trust, and all the negativity that makes life impossible. As soon as one walks into a house one can sense the atmosphere and know whether we have entered the portals of heaven or hell. It is so easy to see, so impossible to hide, for the very air cries out its protest against us when we sin. As Jesus taught us these signs represent two distinctly different kingdoms with different frames of reference, different fruits and different destinies beyond the grave. Let us remind ourselves again of the words of Moses in Deuteronomy 30.15–20: "see, today I set before you life and prosperity, death and disaster. If you obey the commandments of the Lord your God . . . if you love the Lord your God and follow His ways . . . you will live and increase, and the Lord your God will bless you in the land that you are entering to make your own. But if your heart strays . . . you will most certainly perish . . . Choose life then, so that you and your descendants may live, in the love of the Lord your God, obeying his voice, clinging to him; for in this your life consists . . ."

The choice to experience heaven or hell lies entirely with ourselves, and we must pay the price, and live out the consequences of that choice. There is no cheap grace, and life offers us opportunities to show what metal we are made of. Life challenges us to be overcomers, not jelly-babies afraid of every whiff of trouble. There is a price to pay for happiness and peace and Jesus showed us the way, for He won our salvation at the price of His precious blood, terrible torture, and death. Let us look to him now as our model, and see the choice that He made; what life offered Him in exchange for His love; what He did about hurts, rejection, hatred, suspicion, accusations, including false accusations. But first let us look at His teaching on forgiveness.

PETER'S STRUGGLE WITH FORGIVENESS

Jesus' teaching is clear and unambiguous. If you want to stay in right relationship with God you must forgive – always, and under all circumstances. Peter was called to take the shepherd's role in Jesus' place after the crucifixion, so it was imperative that he would understand the mind of his Master. So he questioned Him in Matthew 18.21–22. "Lord" he said, "how often must I forgive my brother if he wrongs me? As much as seven times"? Jesus answered, "Not seven, I tell you, but seventy times seven". I'm sure Peter was sorry that he asked, for now he could no longer plead ignorance!

Peter lived in a fishing village called Bethsaida on the shores of Lake Galilee where he worked as a fisherman. The poor people there literally lived almost on top of each other, in difficult political, social and religious circumstances. They had to pay exorbitant taxes on everything, and there was no one to take their case to any tribunal. Their country was governed by Rome, whose occupying forces they all hated. There was terrible injustice everywhere, in commerce, social life, religious and political life. And Peter hears that he must go back to them with this crazy teaching about forgiveness! He could expect to be lynched by people who were overwrought by the burdens of life, for giving way to hatred at least ventilated their great frustrations.

And then there was the simple fact that Peter was a man of the world, and knew how human beings operated. He knew, as we all do, that whole families often break up just because of *one* hurt, let alone seven. How many families break up over a will? How many families carry on feuds for generations so that the present encumbents don't even know *why* they are warring? It's just traditional! Such was the case between the Jews and the Samaritans who mutually hated each other. That did not mean that any *particular* Samaritan had hurt *you* but you kept up the tradition of hatred anyway. Such is the case today between Protestants and Catholics in the North of Ireland, and in Scotland, where loyalty to one's own "side" demands it! Then what about political hatreds that can be carried on for millenia, like apartheid and anti-Semitism? Truly when one considers the way human beings behave Jesus' teaching on forgiveness seems naïve, to say the least. And who obeys it? Apart from the few saints whom we smile benignly at because they are "different"?

Peter's problem was *real*. And it is our problem today if we wish to participate in bringing the solution to the human race, and that solution is peace on earth. Let's take this problem on a personal level before we even think it could be operated to serve the human race as a whole. When someone hurts you it cuts deep into the emotions, and can be hard to eradicate. In obedience to the Lord you forgive and try to deal with the emotional healing, and the issues at stake.

Then it happens again, and this time the hurt sits on a recent emotional wound, which means that it hurts *more* than the last time, and one feels betrayed and misused. It is more difficult to forgive now. It requires more courage, more grace, more energy, and more perseverance. But when it happens a third time . . . a fourth . . . fifth . . . sixth! Can you see Peter's problem? He realizes that by then you would be emotionally distraught, and your marriage or whatever the relationship involved would be in shambles. Maybe you would be in shreds too! Could you stretch it to that perfect time? Jesus asks here for heroic love. Something that only God can give us the ability to give, and persevere with, something we would most likely need help to achieve.

Peter's problem is that he wants to put a ceiling on Jesus' teaching on forgiveness. If someone goes this far, then after that no forgiveness, just hand them over to the Law. Oh! how often we have felt that way ourselves! Human nature can stretch very little. It cries out get even. The logic of forgiving Jesus' way can bypass us completely. Human nature cries out: "But it's not

fair! Why should he get away with it all the time? I'm the one that's hurt. Surely it is his turn to do something? Why does it always have to be me? He has the same obligation to forgive and repent as I have. It's not fair!" In an "eye for an eye and a tooth for a tooth" world it certainly is *not fair*!

DIVINE WISDOM

Jesus' response to the problem was given in a dramatic parable. It is the story of the unforgiving debtor in Matthew 18.23–35. In His wisdom Jesus realized that some things are understood better when we *feel* them rather than hearing them as dry doctrine. This is one of the reasons why He taught in parables, because we could enter into the story, and experience the issues, and thus understand them better.

This story concerns a king who was having a day of reckoning with his subjects who were indebted to him. So we must picture a huge hall where the king sits on his throne in royal splendour surrounded by his ministers of state, while the poor servants are arraigned before him for judgment because of unpaid debts. It would be a terrifying experience for an ordinary workman, and he would realize that there was no court of appeal. Whatever sentence was given by the king was his fate, and it would be carried out immediately. (This is Matthew's image of the Final Judgment at the end of the world also. See Matthew 25.31–46).

Out of the whole morning's business only two cases are cited. One is that of a man who owed his king the equivalent of £3,000,000, so it was impossible to pay it back. The other is the case of a man who owed the first man (not the king) three months' wages, which he *could* pay back. The drama is played out between these two men. The sum of money owed by the first man is outrageously large, and it is obvious that the king represents God, and this sum of money represents our inability to *pay God* what we owe Him due to our sinfulness. This is what we quoted from Psalm 49.7–8 before: "But man could never redeem himself, or pay his ransom to God: it costs too much to redeem his life, it is beyond him . . . ."

The king gave the sentence. The man was to be sold into slavery, together with his wife and children in order to repay some of what was owed. And all the man's possessions would revert to the crown also. The man knew that he was finished, as good as dead. What is more he realized that he brought this terrible fate to those he loved also! In sheer desperation he threw himself at the king's feet and implored *mercy*. Justice had already been pronounced, and *that* was intolerable. The only hope lay in the king's merciful heart, and he was known for his merciful love.

The king felt compassion for the man. This means that he was mentally able to put himself into the man's shoes, and thus feel his pain. The result of this exercise was that the king *forgave him the entire debt!* One moment the man was destined to slave labour for the whole of his life, then the next he was a free man. And not only that, but he had *no debt at all* to pay now! This is incredible. The forgiveness was so total that even the king's *just dues* were cancelled. It must have been almost impossible to grasp such an act of love. Surely we would expect this man would be *so touched* by the king's generosity that it would be the model for his own behaviour. Surely he can see that it would be *unjust* for him to behave in any other way, since the people who hurt us are usually unable *to do anything about it*. In a vast number of cases they cannot undo the damage. Only your forgiveness can take the harm out of a bad situation.

Let us see if he is prepared to pass on to others what was given so magnificently to him. The story goes on to say that when this man went out from the king's presence that he *happened* to meet someone who owed *him* three months' wages. Will he be merciful, now that he knows what it feels like to *receive* mercy? No! He grabbed the poor man by the throat and began to throttle him, demanding his money. His neighbour threw himself on his knees – obviously when he managed to get out of the vice grip – and begged for time, for he had every intention of repaying the loan. He wondered what was the problem? Didn't the man know that he intended to pay it back? Why the sudden urgency? But the forgiven man would not listen, and had his neighbour handed over to the law officers to be put into prison until he paid the debt. My dear reader, how *do you* feel about this man's behaviour? Do you feel angry? Do you think that he was *unjust*? Even in a tit-for-tat world he should have had the decency to let his neighbour free of his debt, since he himself was let off.

The onlookers to this drama were so angry when the forgiven man would not himself forgive others, that they reported the whole matter to the king, who now did to him what he had done to his neighbour! But with this exception: in the first instance the king had not condemned this servant for his debt. He had merely sentenced him according to the law. But now he condemns him also. Then the master sent for him. "You wicked servant", he said. "I cancelled all that debt of yours when you appealed to me. Were you not bound then, to have pity on your fellow servant just as I had pity on you?". And in his anger the master handed him over to the torturers til he should pay all his debt. And that is how my heavenly Father will deal with you unless you each forgive your brother from your heart (Matt. 18.32–35).

It is only with this illustration that we can understand the logic of forgiveness, or the justice of it either. Jesus tells us that we must keep in mind just how much God has forgiven us, and what the implications of that forgiveness are for us eternally, and then we will pass this incredible gift on to others and be a participant in their redemption. When we are called upon to forgive we are asked to portray the face and heart of God to others for their salvation. Like the Master we are called upon to overcome evil with good.

THE FALL AND RISE OF PETER

Unfortunately we do not learn well theoretically, but we do remember what we have experienced. Peter learned how to proclaim this divine forgiveness to the world by experiencing it! So let us look at the fall and rise of our beloved Peter, the one called to shepherd the flock in the footsteps of the Master. There is no shred of doubt that Peter loved Jesus. With all the impulsiveness and enthusiasm of his soul he threw himself into the ministry of Jesus, often tripping both himself and Jesus up with his ability to act before thinking first. Such an occasion was when he wanted to prevent Jesus from suffering – because he loved Him! "Heaven preserve you Lord", he said. "This must not happen to you". The poor man had to take a very severe rebuke from his beloved Master on that occasion: "Get behind me, Satan! You are an obstacle to my path, because the way you think is not God's way, but man's" (Matt. 16.21–23). It would take some doing for Peter to get over his feelings on this one, but he did, and they went on.

The crunch point came when this suffering that Peter *really did not want* for his Master, came to pass. Peter had taken the rebuke on the chin, but had not changed his mind on the necessity of suffering if Jesus was to redeem the world. To change one's way of thinking on a particular subject is the meaning of *repentance*, and since Peter has not repented, the Passion of Jesus becomes a time for entering into temptation for the disciple. Moreover, we are told that both he and the other male disciples had not obeyed Jesus on the question of prayer either, so they entered the garden of Gethsemane unprepared for the crisis that was facing them. Jesus prayed there but they did not. They took refuge in sleep (see Mark 13.33–37; Matt. 26.36–46).

Then disaster struck. The Master was arrested and taken off in chains. Of course Peter tried to defend Him, according to his human way of thinking, which the Master did not want. He took out a sword hidden in his cloak and struck the High Priest's servant, cutting off his ear (John 18.10–11). What this was meant to achieve I'm sure not even Peter knew! It was just that impulsiveness again, but he had said at the Supper that he would defend Jesus. Peter said, "though all lose faith in you, I will never lose faith". Jesus answered him, "I tell you solemnly, this very night, before the cock crows, you will have disowned me three times". Peter said to him, "Even if I have to die with you, I will never disown you". And all the disciples said the same (Matt. 26.33–35). But that was before the event.

With the arrest of Jesus confusion set in, yet curiosity

made Peter follow to see what would happen to the Master. However, it was no longer an advantage to be recognized as a disciple if Jesus was condemned. And He was! Condemned by the High Priest and the Sanhedrin, who decided to hand Him over to Pilate. What now? Peter thought that he could hide in the anonymous crowd, thought he would not be recognized. This is the temptation of Christians during persecution or an era of unbelief such as the one we are going through just now, when it is no longer "the thing" to be seen to be a friend of Jesus. There is no credit for believing when everybody else believes, but what about now when it costs?

Peter's first sin was that he was ashamed of his Master. His second one was that he did not raise his voice in protest to give witness to the innocence of the victim. This amounted to a denial of Jesus in public. Thirdly, he allied himself with "the world", and warmed himself at its worldly fire, whereas he should have stayed faithful to Jesus and the fire of the Holy Spirit, which would have given him wisdom and strength to deal with the situation, in grace.

Then, as luck would have it, he was recognized! A servant girl recognized him as a disciple, and his fourth sin was that he denied discipleship, pretending that he did not know what she was talking about. But she persevered, and someone else recognized even his accent. Under the pressure of scrutiny Peter lost his head altogether, and cursed and swore that he never knew Jesus (Mark 14.66–72). This was his fifth sin. The prodigal son was down now, and out! It was then, at that psychological moment, that Jesus, who was undergoing a very unjust trial Himself, turned and caught Peter's attention with His eyes, and mediated His loving mercy to His erring disciple (Luke 22.61).

Peter broke under the strain of so much love and went out and wept his way to repentance and freedom. The firey, impulsive Simon Bar Jona died that night, and the new Peter was born, a monument to God's grace, the new rock on which Jesus could depend in building His Church (Matt. 16–18). This rock emerged from the womb of forgiveness, and an edifice of God's making was to be built on forgiveness alone! Every living stone in the New Temple would be remade by this divine thing, transforming the most unlikely material into a house fit for God Himself, a house made by Himself, *all of grace* (I Pet. 2.4–10). Salvation comes to us wrapped in God's loving forgiveness.

Forgiveness was Jesus' secret weapon for overcoming evil, and transforming the world, by transforming the human heart with this overflowing love. "Yes, God loved the world so much that he gave his only Son, so that everyone who believes in him may not be lost but may have eternal life. For God sent his Son into the world not to condemn the world, but so that through him the world might be saved." Jesus had to die to make Peter a rock, and also to make us into living stones in His Temple. It was costly grace, but was it worth it? Yes.

But let us go back to Peter on the night of his fall. He had the terrible weight on his heart that when Jesus needed him most he was unavailable. He had been "all mouth". His promises to Jesus had meant nothing. His words were just "hot air" with no reality behind them. Now he must see the sight of his beloved Master so cruelly treated, and it is too late to help. Remorse is a dreadful thing, and can drive a person crazy. Does Peter realize at long last that Jesus must die to save *him?*

Holy Saturday must have been the longest day in

Peter's life. His Master was dead and buried, and the male disciples were in the upper room, locked away for fear the Jewish leaders would look for their blood now. All heroism was gone. There was just the stark reality that without Jesus they could do nothing (John 15.5). However, it was not the police who disturbed their reveries, but Mary of Magdala, announcing the Resurrection! The women had seen Jesus risen from the dead, but the person *who needed to see Jesus* was Peter! What was he to do now? Go back to fishing? Would Jesus actually *want* the likes of him in his group, let alone leading it? There was so much to clear up. What was he to do? Luke tells us very simply that "the Lord has risen and has appeared to Simon" (Luke 24:35). No explanation. That meeting was so precious to Peter, that for once he never spoke about it! It was one thing for him to know in his heart that Jesus had forgiven him, but now *he knows*. Whatever went on was too private for public viewing, and speaks of divine love and mercy conquering a soul for ever, and planting the glorious gift of humility there that would protect grace in the future.

PUBLIC RECONCILIATION

Peter was satisfied that things were now settled between himself and the Lord. His debt of £3,000,000 had been wiped off the books. He now knew what that *felt like*. He knew just how freeing it was to experience forgiveness, and the other Apostles accepted Peter's leadership with the same simplicity as before, for hadn't they all let Jesus down? Not even John, the Beloved Disciple, had defended his Master! No! They were all in the same boat with regard to Him. They all

needed His forgiveness. There was no boast on anyone's lips.

Peter would have settled for this, but Jesus knew human nature better than that, so we read in John 21 that after the miraculous catch of fish in Galilee, Jesus made Himself known to all the disciples who were out fishing, when He invited them to a meal on the shore. Then He challenged Peter in front of them all, a triple challenge to wipe out the triple denial: "Simon, son of John, do you love me MORE than these others do?" He answered, "Yes, Lord, you know I love you." Jesus said to him "Feed my lambs". A second time he said to him, "Simon, son of John, Do you LOVE me?" He replied, "Yes, Lord, YOU KNOW I love you". Jesus said to him, "Look after my sheep". Then he said to him a third time, "Simon, son of John, Do you love me?" Peter was upset . . . he said, "Lord, YOU KNOW EVERYTHING; you know I love you". Jesus said to him, "Feed my sheep".

What was going on? Why did Jesus insist on a public reconciliation? Surely He had forgiven Peter. Let us remember that Jesus is incarnate love, so everything that He does is done in love, and for a loving purpose. One of the greatest lessons on the real nature of forgiveness is to be revealed now. If you forgive someone you must treat them as if nothing had gone wrong and you must reinstate them to their former position. Jesus had to show the disciples, and the future Church that when He forgave, the matter was over, and the files were destroyed. Peter was the leader of the Apostles before this event, and Jesus insisted on making sure that this continued after it. He would not allow the matter to be thrown up into Peter's face to torture him, and to cause dissension in the Church, where some people would hold that Peter was unfit for the position because of what he had done. Jesus knew that human beings can be both devious and vicious when ambition takes hold.

Moreover Jesus knew that Peter was *different* as a result of this experience, hence the question that must have surprised them all: "Do you love me MORE than these others do?" They would have said that Peter loved Jesus LESS than all the others! After all, he did curse and swear that he never knew Jesus! But they have forgotten something vital, which Jesus taught and illustrated in the forgiveness of the sinful woman in Luke 7. 36–50. "There was once a creditor who had two men in his debt . . ." (It's the same parable that we have used above, although given in different circumstances) . . . "one owed him 500 denarii and the other 50. They were unable to pay, so he pardoned them both. WHICH OF THEM WILL LOVE HIM MORE?" "The one who was pardoned more I suppose", answered Simon (the Pharisee). Jesus said, "You are right".

Jesus taught that we are all sinners in relation to God, and whether we have sinned greatly or not according to human reckoning, we cannot redeem ourselves. God forgives us according to His divine mercy, not according to our supposed merits. But which one would be the more grateful, and therefore love Him more? Jesus said, and history attests the truth of what He said, namely, that the great sinners who allowed Jesus to redeem them are the very ones who became the GREAT saints, because of *their great love*. Gospel examples are Mary of Magdala and Peter, and afterwards Paul.

Peter's love for Jesus went into an altogether new

51

category once he experienced the pure, unfathomable depths of Jesus' love. This fitted him out to be a *good shepherd* in the likeness of his Master, one who would mediate God's infinite mercy and compassion to sinners. He now understood one of the *keys of the kingdom of God*, for only God knew how to unlock the disasters of the world, and replace them with love, light and life. Forgiveness unlocks those apparently impossible situations between people and nations, ensuring that life can continue on Planet Earth. The alternative is that we obliterate each other.

This public reconciliation of Peter and Jesus was a most important revelation to the Church and the world. Jesus' Easter Proclamation URBI ET ORBI is *"Forgive to live!"*

A TRUE STORY OF FORGIVENESS

Before we bring our discussion to a close I would like to share with you the story of Veronica. It is a true story but the names and circumstances have been changed to protect the participants. It concerns two women who were related to each other, and who, therefore, had all the emotional ties and deep feelings that go with blood relationship and family loyalty. The saga began with Mary's decision to make a significant change in her personal circumstances, a fact absolutely rejected by Veronica, who refused even to discuss the subject. Veronica felt (wrongly) that it was a slight on herself and her family, and ended by rejecting Mary altogether. The situation was complicated by the need for Mary's access to an ageing mother. This simple senario set the stage for a four-year drama that permanently affected both their lives, and afterwards, gave so much hope to others who took courage from hearing it.

Mary was a committed Christian, and sought refuge in prayer for her hurt feelings. She wanted to obey the Lord, but did not know what to do specifically, in this case. She spoke to God in prayer: "Lord, what am I to do? What can I do? I can't make her think differently. And anyway, I am the one who is hurt, not her!" Back from the Lord came the uncompromising reply: "Forgive her. Forgive her from the heart, not from the lips, and then I can work." So Mary spent some time building herself up in prayer where she found the strength and the courage to let go of her feelings, and accept Veronica's rejection in peace.

As soon as Mary was ready the Lord told her to visit her ageing parent. She went, only to find herself left on the doorstep with a tirade of abuse, aware that the eyes of neighbours were watching behind lace curtains. Her humiliation was complete, when access to the parent was denied also. She turned away much more hurt than previously, as this wound sat on the other very recent one. As she put her hand to the garden gate to go away, she heard the Lord say: "Forgive! Forgive from the heart. Don't go past the gate without forgiving. As you open the gate, open your heart to love. . . . "Lord", Mary said, "I can only do it for your sake. I could kill her, I am so angry!" In the silence of the journey home Mary was aware that the Lord was whispering *very gently* that this response was okay for now, but that in future, He hoped that she could rise to actually loving her neighbour! Mary, of course, did not think that this was a bit fair, and refused to discuss the subject further!

Nevertheless, she sought refuge in prayer again. What else could she do? Where could she go? There was no one but the Lord, and He sounded as if He sympathized with "the other side"! After some time of healing and strengthening, the cycle started again with

the usual: "Visit your parent" signal, which Mary knew only spelled more flagellation. And she was right. This went on. . . . and on . . . and on, for four long years. The cycle was rejection, abuse, forgiveness, healing, etc. until it seemed that the treadmill would never end.

Was anything happening during this time? Was it all for nothing? No. So much happened, but so quietly that even Mary did not notice, for she was so concerned with her own responses that she forgot to look for changes on the "other side" until she was nudged to do so by the Lord! It was only then that she noticed the atmosphere had changed quietly. The rejection had continued but the abuse had ceased. She was amazed to notice that her own feelings had changed completely. She was no longer hurt. She did not even pity Veronica. She just prayed for her good, in peace. She was no longer tempted to say to the Lord: "Bless her . . . but with a brick!" (A fact that she had consoled herself was just "a concrete sign of affection!") She really meant that she wanted blessing and grace for her opponent.

Somehow the situation was completely different now. Mary was free emotionally, and realized that God had done her a great service. He had used this situation to build her a wonderful fortress where the fiery darts of the enemy of souls could not penetrate. She had quietly moved out of Chronos-time where the world dictates, to Kairos-time, God's time, where God works in his vineyard according to His laws, which concern Redemption. Already this was a good fruit to reap from the forgiveness, but God's generosity is infinite, so there was much more to come.

The next stage was a revelation for Mary, one that made her laugh at herself and become more free than ever. She realized with a flash of understanding that she was not God's gift to humanity, and that it was okay for Veronica, or anyone else, not to like her or what she did! This may seem trivial, but it was very liberating. So what, if someone rejects you and does not agree with you! Life does not end there. Life marches on. So what if someone abuses you? That only reflects where THEY are at. It does not necessarily reflect where you are at in anything. Allow others their freedom to respond to life as they wish. Just pray for them, love and serve them as circumstances permit. We don't have to go into negativity for life just because we have had a bit of a to-do with someone.

This emotional freedom of course meant that Veronica lost the power to hurt Mary. It was like taking the sword out of her hand and breaking it. Mary arrived one day to find herself accepted quietly, and access was given to the parent. Of course the poor mother was distraught, thinking she had a permanent rift in the family. Imagine her surprise when Mary turned up in her room, and smiling!

Imagine her amazement when Mary did not need to complain or grumble, but instead knelt in front of the mother and said: "Jesus told us that if two of us agreed, with one mind and heart over something that he would give it to us (Matt. 18.19–20. This text comes just before the teaching on forgiveness!). Will you agree with me to unite your pain for Veronica with mine, and both of us unite our pain with that of Jesus, our crucified and glorious Saviour, and offer this to God for her conversion?" The mother agreed to the deal, and also to keep silence on the subject. Since she was housebound, Mary assured her that she should not worry if the visits were infrequent. It did not indicate an absence of love. The mother was so relieved that she began to feel better, and move about more.

The final stage came when Mary turned up for another visit only to find a smiling Veronica greet her at the door, invite her in, and offer her coffee! As Veronica prepared the refreshments Mary prayed desperately for help, because she was so used to the problem, that she had no idea what to do with a healing! The coffee was a good distraction as Veronica began her story of the past four years. She told Mary how she had *literally willed her* to hate, for that would have given Veronica justification for how she had reacted. But when Mary refused to hate, Veronica only hated her even more, and desperately wanted to hurt her. Hence she had controlled the visits to the mother, and added abuse and rejection. When Mary seemed impervious to hurt, Veronica stopped and took a good look at herself and realized how horrible a person she had become, and that it was all her own doing! But now she had repented, confessed her sin to the Lord, and she wanted Mary's forgiveness. . . . and she asked for it on her knees!

Mary was deeply moved as Veronica told her that she had seen the face and heart of Christ in her, and in her behaviour over the past four years. "You have been a true icon", she said. "You should be called Veronica, not me!" Slowly Mary got the courage to tell her side of the story. If Veronica was moved before, she was speechless now as she learned the cost of forgiveness. All the time she had told herself, "Oh well. Mary is just like that." She did not allow herself to see that Mary was indeed suffering.

Now she had to listen to the terrible struggle not to hate, not give tit-for-tat, either in speech or action. Mary was not the "goody-goody" that she had labelled her, but a friend of Jesus prepared to pay the cost of discipleship. Veronica felt very humbled when Mary confessed: "I thought that I was a good Christian, but that was before I was tested. You showed me just how superficial my commitment to Christ and His way really was. Veronica, I want to thank you for forcing me to become a real disciple of Jesus!".

The surprise of this story is that it is about two "baddies", not one, just like the story of the prodigal son. Yet each in her own way, and at her own stage, was open to learn, and God used one diamond to cut another! Since diamond is the hardest substance known, He had to use an immovable thing to get Mary to move on spiritually. As the Book of Proverbs says: Iron is made the finer by iron, a person is refined by contact with his neighbour. The Lord, in His wisdom had used these two people to sandpaper each other into sanctity! And they say that God does not have a sense of humour!

My reader, ask yourself has God given you a Veronica? If so, please do not complain about your privileges. The Lord is interested in your growth, and is providing the opportunity for that. The hardest bit is to recognize Veronica. Once that is done, it is relatively easy to go to the Lord and begin your adventure. Bon Voyage!

UNCONQUERABLE BENEVOLENCE

Let us complete our contemplation of forgiveness by looking at Jesus Himself, in order to feel the gentle breath of His divine loving-kindness that transforms our hells into paradise. Jesus *IS FORGIVENESS*. He is incarnate love, dispersing the perfume of paradise everywhere He goes. His whole public ministry can be put under the heading of forgiveness, for He came to mediate this heavenly gift to anyone who is open to God and life, and salvation.

Jesus went out of His way to find the outcasts of society. He took what others called "the dregs" and transformed them into saints and missionaries. In fact he turned the whole world upside down with these transformed characters whom nobody could squash, because they wanted the world's dregs to experience the glory offered to them. Jesus gave forgiveness where Israel only offered condemnation and death. Such were the cases of the prostitutes and public sinners, whom the law would have killed. But Jesus called them, forgave them, healed them, transformed them, and through them brought the kingdom of God on earth.

All this is wonderful and we love to read these stories in the gospel. But what happened to Jesus Himself? Was He accepted? Was His background accepted? Was His doctrine accepted? He forgave, but was He forgiven for coming from Nazareth? For being poor? For being uneducated? For holding out against the accepted taboos of the day? For not limiting His behaviour to the ignorance of the time? Oh No! He was not forgiven. He was mocked and jeered at for being a country Rabbi who had not passed through "the system". He was laughed at for having uneducated disciples (although some of them were educated), for only having the mob as His followers. The mighty ones of the land had no time for Him, although they were jealous of His giftedness and power to heal.

Worse than that, the Pharisees and scribes followed Him about picking holes in everything He said and did. They were so angry at His changing obsolete rules without referring to them, that they twisted His words and accused Him of all kinds of things. Among the accusations they flung at Him were these: that He was a glutton and a wine-bibber because He presented Himself as ordinary, not as extraordinary, like John the Baptist. They said that he was possessed by Satan, and that He did His exorcisms through Satan's power. They accused Him of being a Sabbath breaker, which to them was serious. Also that He was an enemy of Caesar, and a prophet who stirred up the people with false teaching.

If you were the Son of God how would you feel about this, since you had come down from heaven specially to save the people? Would you feel hurt? Rejected? Spat upon? I think so! Would you FEEL like redeeming them? How do you feel when your family or friends treat you this way? Does it make you want to do great things for them? Jesus must have been tempted to behave like the God of Sinai towards them. That is, he must have felt like judging them instead of redeeming them. And the world is no different today.

The leaders of Israel were probably unaware just how difficult they made things for Jesus. In the end He cried over Jerusalem that had rejected the greatest divine visitation the world would ever know (Luke 19.41–44). And yet, in spite of this He went on to give His life for the very people who rejected Him and they still did not thank Him! They were just glad to get rid of a nuisance, so that they could go back to "normality" whatever that was.

Jesus' whole ministry could be described in terms of "binding and loosing". He had come to set the captives free (Luke 4.18), and to unbind everyone from their bondages, whether material or spiritual. (It is important to note here that the real meaning of forgiveness is to unbind someone and let them go free.) He unbound the lepers from their leprosy, and the sick from their sickness. He unbound the prostitutes from their slavery to the body, and the tax collectors from their slavery to money. He unbound the sinners from their slavery to sin, and even unbound the cords of death itself. But wickedness got to work against Him, spurred on by Satan, the master of all wickedness.

Nevertheless, when Jesus surrendered to His enemies in the Garden of Gethsemane they bound Him, and held Him captive until death. Was the merciful one shown any mercy? Was the forgiving one shown any forgiveness? Was the loving one shown any love? No, for human beings are so cruel to each other. Man's inhumanity to man is one of the greatest mysteries we have to deal with here on earth.

They did for Him the exact opposite of what He had done for others. Once physically bound, they then tried to bind Him emotionally through torture and an unjust trial on trumped-up charges, which were changed to suit the changing circumstances of Pilate's court. Then he was nailed to His cross until he died. He who had unbound others died bound to the cross. Was that fair? Was this the way to treat the benefactor of the human race? The only one who could save us from our sins? The only one who could do anything about our hell problem? Isn't it crazy when the sick kill the only doctor alive? It's not fair!

How did Jesus react? Did He reject when he was rejected? Did He give tit-for-tat? Did He abuse verbally or otherwise? No! He stood silent before His accusers, only speaking when forced to do so under oath. He kept an attitude of humble respect before the legitimate leaders of "Church" and State. At the same time He kept His dignity and personal freedom, so that no torture could wring from Him any response that He did not want to give. His attitude before such injustice was nothing short of regal dignity, and nothing that was done to Him removed this royalty from Him. It only proved it, for it was His own executioner, the Centurion, who said as soon as He breathed His last: "In truth this man was a son of God" (Mark 15.39).

As He hung dying in excruciating pain, Jesus managed to find excuses for His murderers: "Father, forgive them; they do not know what they are doing." In a very real sense they DID know what they were doing! They had deliberately stage-managed His passion and death, and their triumph was to see Him die an ignominious death. Yet Jesus was right. In an even greater sense, if their eyes were truly opened to who He was, they would never have crucified the Lord of Glory (I Cor. 2.8). Only blind eyes could do such a deed, and that is the excuse for forgiveness.

What unconquerable love! What greatness of soul! What a man! What a Saviour! What terrifying humility of our God! Let us tremble in His presence, ask for enlightenment, and obey His command to love at any cost.

One final word: please remember that when people hurt us there is a very real sense in which it is true that they do not know what they are doing. Sure they realize that they are hurting you, but most of them would never consciously want the emotional damage that can be caused. Very often the people who hurt others are hurting themselves, and they hit out from that unhealed area of their lives. Is it possible that after contemplating Jesus we, too, could say: "Father, forgive them, *they don't realise what they are doing?*" If we can do that, then we are the privileged ones that have the earth for our heritage, and the kingdom of God is ours too. What a treasure!